D1452862

True Stories of Exceptional Character

VOLUME 1

BY THE BIBLE
TELLS ME SO
PRESS

True Stories of Exceptional
Character, Volume 1

A collection of stories
compiled and illustrated
by The Bible Tells Me So Press

ISBN 13: 978-0-692-06123-7

PUBLISHED BY
THE BIBLE TELLS ME SO CORPORATION
1122 CRESCENT AVE, SUITE C
ANAHEIM, CA 92801
WWW.THEBIBLETELLSMESO.COM

First Printing January 2018

Table of Contents

Preface

In our first volume we wish to explore 5 exceptional character traits: trustworthiness, bravery, honesty, forgiving, and believing. First we see Charles shine above his peers in his new job. Then Abbie faces a dreadful storm alone without her father. Next Bobby stuns the whole school, and Corrie faces someone from her awful past. And finally, we look in on George Müller as he provides breakfast for 300 orphans. In each of these true stories, we can be impressed with the exceptional patterns of character that each one demonstrates.

CHAPTER ONE

Mr. Brown Finds a Boy He Can Trust

Have you ever had to trust someone to do something very important for you? Maybe your teacher assigned a group project at school, and it required everyone to do their part or you all would get a bad grade. Yes, being trustworthy is an exceptional character trait that we all appreciate. In this true story, we'll get to know three boys and find out which one is trustworthy.

Three boys lived in America many years ago: Joe, Henry and Charles. They grew up together, were in the same class in school, and were very good friends.

When they got to the age of fourteen, Joe and Henry began to go out at nights and didn't bother with studying. Charles stayed at home and studied for the lessons the next day. Of course the difference showed up in their schoolwork, and Joe and Henry began to fall behind. When examination time came the boys begged Charles to help them cheat.

The boys begged Charles to help them cheat.

"No," said Charles firmly. "I will never do anything like that. My mother told me that my father wanted me to be honest, and I mean to be."

"Come on! Your parents will never know," said Henry.

"Yeah, you could give your friend some help in his examination," grumbled Joe.

"That would be cheating, or helping you to cheat, which would be just as bad," said Charles quietly, turning away to get on with his own work.

Charles passed all the examinations with honors, and Joe and Henry failed. From then on they began to torment Charles, calling him names, and shouting after him, "Mommy's honest little darling!"

Charles' mother knew something was wrong and asked him what the problem was. Charles squirmed uncomfortably and sighed. He took a deep breath and told his mother all that had happened. Her face brimmed with care, and she said how proud she was of him. "I will never be ashamed of you as long as you are honest. It may be hard sometimes, but you will see in a few years it really pays."

Charles felt encouraged again and could face the boys. He looked them straight in the eyes, without being afraid or ashamed. Joe and Henry then dropped their eyes and didn't bother him again. Actually, the head teacher had heard of their actions, and they had been punished.

As the school holidays approached, the boys wanted to earn some money. One day, Henry was passing a shop with a notice in the window saying, "Help wanted. Apply

Mr. Brown asked him to sort some nuts and bolts.

in person." We don't know the shop-keeper's name, but we'll call him "Mr. Brown." Henry asked about the job, and Mr. Brown took him to the back of the store and assigned him to sort some nuts and bolts.

After a while, Henry appeared suddenly and said, "What a boring job! If that's all you have for me to do, I don't want the job anymore." Mr. Brown paid him for the work he had done, and Henry slipped out the door to go home.

When Mr. Brown looked in the back room where Henry was work-ing, he found all the nuts and bolts were still scattered all over the floor. He picked them up himself and put the notice for a helper back in the window.

The next day, Joe saw the notice and went in to ask for the job. Mr. Brown gave him the same work to do, sorting the nuts and bolts. After a while Joe burst into Mr. Brown's office and gasped, "Oh, why don't you just throw this junk away? I don't like this job anymore. I quit." Again, Mr. Brown paid Joe for his work and said to himself, "I am willing to pay more than this to find someone I can trust."

A few days later, as Henry and Joe passed the shop, they discussed what a boring job it was. Then with a smirk, Joe asked Henry, "Hey, did you find anything interesting in those old boxes besides the nuts and bolts?"

Henry looked at Joe and laughed, "Well, if I did, I'm not telling you." Joe was a little alarmed to hear this and thought to himself, "I wonder if he found the same thing I did?" But Joe didn't say anything as they just kept walking down the street together.

One day, Charles also passed Mr. Brown's shop and saw his notice for a helper was still up in the window. So he went in and asked for the job.

"Tell me, Charles, are you friends with Joe and Henry?" asked Mr. Brown.

"Oh! No sir. We used to be, but something happened, and now they won't talk to me."

"Hmm, that's very interesting," replied Mr. Brown, slowly. "Well, if you want the job you can start by sorting these nuts and bolts, please."

Charles got right to work. It took him two or three hours to finish. Every so often he whistled a tune to help encourage himself as he worked diligently. He found some empty boxes and separated the nuts, bolts, and screws neatly into them. After some time Mr. Brown came to find out how he was doing.

Charles exclaimed, "Sir, look what I found at the bottom of all the bolts!" He handed Mr. Brown a five-dollar gold piece. He smiled and gave Charles some other errands to do. In fact, each day that week Charles came back and worked for Mr. Brown.

After a few weeks, Mr. Brown gave Charles the key to the shop, and asked him to come in early and clean before the shop opened. While Charles was sweeping the floor, he found some pennies, and then another time, a dime and a few nickels. Each time, he put them on the shelf and told Mr. Brown about them. Later that week, when Charles received the envelope with his first wages, he was shocked to find the five-dollar gold piece he had found sorting the nuts and bolts was in it!

"Sir, look what I found!"

One morning when Charles was sweeping he found a shiny new dollar coin. How he wished he could keep it for himself! "Mr. Brown would never know," he thought, turning the coin over in his hand. Suddenly he remembered what his mother had said: "I'll never be ashamed of you as long as you are honest." He quickly laid the coin on the shelf, and when the shopkeeper came in he told him about it. Mr. Brown patted him on the shoulder and said, "You see, I really can trust you, Charles." At the end of that week, he was surprised to find that shiny dollar in his wage packet as well!

As time went on the shopkeeper entrusted Charles with large sums of money to take to the bank and gave him even more responsibility in the store. Charles was so pleased

*The shopkeeper entrusted Charles with large
sums of money to take to the bank.*

because he could now help his tired mother by giving her his money at the end of each week. At last she didn't have to work so hard taking extra washing from the neighbors.

"Do you remember the first day you came and sorted all those nuts and bolts?" Mr. Brown asked Charles one day.

"Oh! Yes!" answered Charles. "I was so happy to find work to help my mother, and I'll never forget finding that five-dollar gold piece at the bottom of all those bolts!"

"Well, I think it's time to tell you that I put that gold piece there on purpose. I wanted to find out what sort of boy you were. When you brought it to me I was pretty sure I had finally found a helper I could trust around the shop," said Mr. Brown proudly.

"You did!" exclaimed the astonished Charles.

"Yes, but I wanted to be sure, so I tested you further," Mr. Brown went on. "I also left pennies on the floor and other small coins, and finally, the shiny dollar. When you picked them up and gave them all back to me, I knew I could safely trust you."

"Can I ask you," said Charles as he was remembering these things. "Was there a gold piece lying at the bottom of the bolts when Henry and Joe sorted them?"

"Yes," answered Mr. Brown, "and they both kept it for themselves. I may have lost 10 dollars searching for an honest helper, but it was worth it—for I found one at last."

After some years, what happened to these boys when they grew up? As for Henry and Joe, both of them continued in their dishonest ways. Henry developed a bad habit of stealing as a boy. As a grown man,

Mr. Brown gave him a full-time job in the shop.

he couldn't keep a job. Since he was so dishonest no one could trust him. Joe didn't get into as much trouble as a boy, but when he grew up, he forged a check and was sent to prison. How could he be trusted after that?

But what about Charles? After Charles graduated from school, Mr. Brown gave him a full-time job in the shop. He had certainly found a boy he could trust.

He who is faithful in the least
is faithful also in much;
and he who is unrighteous in the least
is unrighteous also in much.
LUKE 16:10

CHAPTER TWO

Abbie Braves the Storm

Everyone has had times in their life when they were scared. Sometimes a task may seem impossible to accomplish or a situation too difficult to handle. At other times, things may just get downright scary. We all know what it's like to be afraid. That must be why we all recognize bravery as one of those exceptional character traits that we all admire. Here's a story of a courageous young girl who risked her life to save others in this incredible adventure by the sea.

In 1839 on the east coast of the United States, a girl was born named Abbie Burgess. She was the fourth of nine children, and at this time there were still no electric lights and radar, or even weather reports. Her mother was not able to walk, and her father was the lighthouse keeper on Matinicus Rock, a rocky little island situated 18 miles off the coast.

A lighthouse is a very tall and strong building like a big round tower with a glass room on the very top, called the lantern room. Through

A lighthouse is a very tall and strong building.

the glass walls of the lantern room shines a very bright light to warn sailors not to come too close, or their boats could crash on the rocks. What a terrible disaster for all the crew and cargo!

Abbie and her large family lived in a little wooden house right next to the lighthouse. By the time she was 17, she had four chickens and made them a hen house with some wood that had been washed up from the sea. She loved to climb up the lighthouse stairs with her father. They curved up and around and around all the way up to the lantern room at the top. She liked to watch her father clean the reflectors around the lamps and fill the lamps with oil. Then he lit the lamps to make sure the light could be seen shining out through the glass, so that sailors out at sea could see the light from every direction.

It was winter now, and sometimes it was so cold that the windows became covered with thick layers of ice. Her father had to open the door of the lantern room, step out on to a small balcony, and walk around, scraping all the ice off the windows. In the summer it was lovely to stand there on that balcony and watch the seagulls flying past and look far away to the boats out at sea. But now, in the winter time, it was frightening to be on that narrow little walkway with the icy wind blowing so hard.

Around that time, Abbie's father decided that he would have to sail to the mainland to get some supplies. The boat that usually brought provisions had not come and there was not much food left for them to eat.

Her father set sail in their small sailing boat.

Since Abbie's mom could not care for the lamps because of her condition, he sat down with Abbie at the kitchen table. He looked serious.

"Abbie, my dear, I need to sail to the mainland for food and provisions. Can you be brave to look after the lamps for me while I'm away? I will leave tomorrow morning and only be gone for one night."

Abbie bit her lip nervously. Such a responsibility! Even for just one night!

"Yes, dad, I'll do my best," she replied, summoning every ounce of courage she could muster.

Early the next day, her father set sail in their small sailing boat. Little did he know, but later that day one of the biggest storms ever recorded would blow in. As night fell, the wind began to howl, and the rain lashed down harder and harder. Abbie knew what she had to do. Just like she had watched her father do countless times before, she must climb those windy stairs up to the lantern room and light the lamps. If not, in this weather, boats would not be able to see the rocks and be wrecked up against them for sure.

But this time she had to do it alone. She bravely took her lamp and began to climb the stairs. When she reached the top, it was a terrible scene. There was so much noise! The wind and rain howled about and caused everything to creak, shake, and rattle. She leaned forward and quickly polished the reflectors. Then she filled the lamps with oil, being careful not to spill with all the shaking. And now she could light each lamp carefully, just like her father would do. When all the lamps were lit, the room was wonderfully filled with warmth and brightness against the cold harsh night. It was only then that she dared think everything was going to be okay.

Relieved, she turned to look out the windows. Oh no! There was ice all over them! The light was unable to shine through clearly. There was no time to relax now. She knew what she had to do. She remembered how her father would climb out onto that slippery little ledge to clear the ice off the windows. But could she do that all by herself in this freezing wind?

"Yes!" she thought, gathering her courage. "I must do it! Daddy assigned me this to look after the lighthouse. And what about all those poor sailors out there in this terrible storm? Yes, scared or not, I must do it."

Oh no! There was ice all over the windows!

She took a deep breath and pushed against the heavy steel door. She had to use all her strength just to push open the door against the strong wind. Once outside, she began to carefully scrape the ice from the first window. As the icy chunks came loose they rattled down around her feet before falling to the rocks below. Before too long, her hands burned with pain. Window by window, she worked her way around the narrow balcony. Finally, with her hands frozen and numb, she pried the door back open and clamored back inside.

At last she was once again inside the haven of the lantern room. Abbie shook her coat and stomped her boots to get the cold rain and ice off of them. Then she lifted her cold little hands to warm them against the lamps as they seemed to shine right through her into the stormy blackness. She was safe for now. But the storm showed no sign of letting up. Slowly, step by step, she made her way back down the winding staircase to her family.

Her worried mother was waiting for her. And needless to say, no one slept much through that terrible night. In the morning the storm was still raging. Abbie's father could never sail back in such dangerous weather. Day after day the storm pounded their little island. And now, there was very little food left.

At some point, the sea water began to come under the door of their little wooden house. "Oh! My chickens!" cried Abbie. She opened the door and waded out in knee-high water to rescue her chickens before the next big wave washed right over the island. Eventually, the waves came up so high that Abbie and her family had to leave their small house next to the lighthouse and move into the strong lighthouse itself. It was their only way to get safely above the water.

Night after night, the storm howled on. And each night, Abbie faithfully climbed the stairs and lit the lamps. She cleared the ice when the windows were covered. Even when she became very ill with a terrible fever, she kept remembering her father's words that if the lamps were not lit, the boats would be wrecked on the rocks. She knew that she was the only one who could climb those steps and save the lives of so many sailors.

After two miserable weeks the storm finally calmed down, and the sea was calm again. Abbie set about putting things in order and drying out what she could. But her thoughts were occupied with one question: "Would dad be able to get back now?" She repeatedly stopped and scanned across the horizon, hoping to catch a glimpse of his boat.

Suddenly she cried out, "There's his boat! There's daddy's boat! He's back! He's back!" She ran to the house calling out the good news. By now, Abbie and her family were weak and without food. The little boat seemed to grow larger as it approached, and Abbie scrambled down the rocky path to help pull the boat up to shore. She gave her father a great big hug. How happy they were to see each other again!

After hearing her story, Abbie's father was so proud of his daughter for her bravery. While he was on the mainland, he had heard of many sailors who were in their boats through that terrible storm and were able to steer their ships clear from the rocks because of the light from the lighthouse. How they were grateful for what Abbie had done! Her bravery surely saved many lives in that storm. As a tribute to her bravery, Abbie's name and story were recorded in the history of the lighthouse.

How happy they were to see each other again!

What a brave girl to consider other people and take care of her responsibility, even when she was hungry and ill. While so many stormy nights had passed, she kept the lamps shining so the ships could turn to avoid the dangerous rocks and bring themselves and their passengers safely home to their families. How good it was that on that rocky island, little Abbie had braved the storm.

So that being of good courage, we say, The Lord is my Helper, and I will not fear.

HEBREWS 13:6

CHAPTER THREE

Bobby's Honest Record

Do you have trouble being honest sometimes? Yes, of course, we all know that everyone has told a lie sometime or another. Some lies may seem little, while others may seem like they are big ones that we will remember our whole lives. Whether we are honest or not is a very im-

portant part of who we are. It comes from deep in our heart and can form something exceptional in our character. In this story let's look in on a young boy striving to fulfill a dream, and yet still demonstrating remarkable honesty.

The day had finally come. That's right! It was the day of the 15 foot rope-climbing test at Bobby's school. For three long years, 14-year-old Bobby had been training to beat the current school record of 2.1 seconds. He was consumed with the challenge, practicing in the gym after school and seeing it in his mind as he imagined the climb. At night he even dreamed of breaking the record. As he practiced year after year it seemed that his whole life depended on doing it. By

Bobby had been training to beat the record.

now his hands were firm and solid, and his arms were tight as a spring.

The rules of the contest were simple. Each boy would have three attempts to climb a 15 foot rope. While they did, the coach stood on the ground with a running stopwatch. The moment they touched the wooden board at the top, he would stop the timer and announce the time.

The crowd in the gym gathered, and finally it came to Bobby's turn. He scampered up the rope on his first attempt, hit the board, and slid down. 2.1 seconds had elapsed. He had tied the record! The crowd cheered, and Bobby brimmed with joy.

But he knew there was more to accomplish. He stretched his arms and positioned himself for the second run. The crowd was leaning in to see what would happen. He lept up the rope, scrambled hand over hand, and descended back down just as quickly. Everyone turned to the coach, anticipating his announcement of the time.

"2 seconds!" bellowed the coach, sending the crowd into a cheering frenzy. It was a new record!

But as the whole class was clapping and calling Bobby's name, the coach leaned down and pulled Bobby over. He began to congratulate Bobby, but then hesitated. He just had a little doubt about something, so he knew he needed to check.

"Bobby," he muttered. "Did you touch the board at the top?"

Bobby stared away, expressionless. The coach seemed unsure in his voice. If Bobby just said "yes," that would be the end of it. The coach would trust his word, and

Coach just had a little doubt about something.

Bobby would have the new record. Bobby closed his eyes. He knew he had just missed touching the board. He had swiped at it, but his fingertips just missed. No one else knew for sure. No one had seen that he missed it. And besides, he was already being cheered as the record breaker. All he had to do now was say one little word, "yes." Then the record he had dreamed of for 3 years would be his. What a fight was going on within him!

Before long, something began to rise up from deep inside. Bobby had been taught by his parents to always tell the truth. He knew that. He knew, even when it is hard to do, you should always tell the truth. This was something basic and right and universal.

The coach lowered his head closer to hear Bobby's response. He looked up at the coach, paused a moment, and then bravely, and honestly, shook his head and said, "no."

Now the coach was usually a tough man, shouting out instructions and arranging the team. But this time tears came to his eyes as he straightened up and quieted everyone down.

"Bobby did not set a record in the rope-climb," he announced with his voice breaking. "But, he has set a much finer record for you and everyone to strive for today. He told the truth, even when it was hard to do."

The crowd rumbled in hushed and surprised tones. Turning to Bobby, he said, "I'm so proud of you. And you know, you still have one more attempt left at the rope-climbing record. Do you want to give it another try?"

Bobby gasped. "That's right!" In the emotion of the moment, he had completely forgotten about his third attempt. "I sure do coach!" he replied.

"Now," the coach instructed, "this time try to focus on starting with a higher jump. If you do, I think you can break this record right now!"

The whole crowd fell silent as Bobby crouched down to give it one last try. "Ready, set, go!" the coach hollered. Up he sprang as high as he could jump, his hands quickly grabbing on to the rope, swinging them hand over hand, pulling himself up quicker than ever before. "Slam!" he hit the top board extra loud and extra strong. And then like lightening, he slid back down the rope. Before he even knew what happened, it was over. Everyone in the whole gym stopped and leaned in for the result.

"1.9 seconds!" shouted the coach in excitement. "He did it!"

The whole gym erupted, as if in unison, with cheers and clapping and shouting Bobby's name. This was not only a new school record, it was a new city record as well, and was perhaps even close to a new national record for a boy his age.

The whole gym erupted with cheers.

But in spite of all that, everyone there that day felt the most amazing thing they witnessed was not Bobby's record-breaking rope climb, but Bobby's record-breaking honesty.

Finally, brothers,
what things are true,
what things are dignified,
what things are righteous,
what things are pure,
what things are lovely,
what things are well spoken of,
if there is any virtue
and if any praise,
take account of these things.

PHILIPPIANS 4:8

CHAPTER FOUR

Corrie Forgives Her Prison Guard

At some point in our lives, we all should have gone to someone else and said we were sorry. This may not seem very easy to do. In fact, we may think that it is easier to forgive someone than it is to apologize to them. But in some situations, such as when we are really hurt by others, it may seem impossible to forgive them. In this amazing story we have just such a case, and it demonstrates the exceptional character trait of forgiveness.

During the second world war, invading armies poured into their neighboring countries and took thousands of innocent people captive. One of these innocent civilians who were wrongly arrested was a woman named Corrie Ten Boom. She and her sister Betsie were cruelly arrested and taken away from their home. They were moved far away to a prison camp in another country. Imagine how terrible and frightening this was!

*The prison guards were very mean to them
and to the other prisoners.*

But it was there, in that prison, where the worst was yet to come. The prison guards were very mean to them and to the other prisoners. They made the prisoners suffer very much by giving them little food and water while demanding that they work hard day in and day out. Sickness was everywhere.

Corrie and Betsie were there in the midst of it all. But they had something not all of the other prisoners had. Corrie and Betsie had the Lord Jesus. The believed in Him and spoke with Him and loved Him in spite of their terrible outward situation. This made them different. How? Well, more than once, Corrie heard her sister praying for the Lord to forgive the guards for what they were doing. That's right! She was not praying that God would punish the guards, but forgive them!

Much time passed in the prison as the sisters endured many difficult things. Sadly, Betsie eventually died in the camp. But, Corrie survived and was able to make it back home upon her release. After some time she began to travel around to many different countries telling people about her experiences in the prison camp. When she did, she always made it a point to speak about the amazing love and forgiveness of the Lord Jesus she witnessed in her dear sister Betsie.

One time, after she had finished speaking, a man approached her. When Corrie saw his face, she was shocked! She recognized him right away. It was one of the guards that had wrongfully imprisoned them and treated them so cruelly! He was actually there and coming straight towards her! Imagine the flurry of

*The sisters endured many
difficult things in the prison.*

feelings and emotions coming up inside her as she looked at his face once again!

This time though, his face was not quite the same. Corrie noticed something was different, very different. It was not as mean and dark as before. No, this time, to her surprise, it was pleasant and shining! This was both reassuring to her as well as puzzling. He came up to Corrie and gently held out his hand to her. He told her that now he too loved the Lord Jesus and believed in Him, just like she. And not only that, he had deeply repented for his terrible past and had experienced that the Lord had truly forgiven him for all he had done!

Whoosh! Immediately, all the memories of the past flooded back into Corrie's mind. All the cruelty of those days in captivity came rushing back. And she remembered her poor sister. At that moment she froze up both inside and out. And though he was kindly extending his hand to her, she just could not lift up her hand to shake it. She just stood there, inwardly struggling in her heart. What was she going to do?

Then, an honest prayer welled up within her, "Lord, I have told so many people about forgiveness. But now I can't forgive! Lord, help me! I really need you!"

After a few moments, she settled down and found her hand raising up, shaking at first, to take his. As she did, her heart was suddenly flooded with love, forgiveness, and joy. In that moment she experienced the very truth she had told so many others about. The forgiveness of the Lord Jesus was the only way to be free from all the hurt and all the

*In that moment she experienced the very truth
she had told so many others about.*

wrong that had happened during the war. The Lord forgave that man after so many years. How precious now, that after so many years, Corrie too could forgive him as well.

Bearing one another
and forgiving one another,
if anyone should have
a complaint against anyone;
even as the Lord forgave you,
so also should you forgive.

COLOSSIANS 3:13

CHAPTER FIVE

Breakfast with Mr. Müller

Have you ever expected the worst to happen? That's right. You roll out of bed in the morning, and everything looks awful. The sky is grey, the cereal is soggy, and that test today in math is going to be a disaster. How wonderful then, if in the middle of all that, you somehow *find the capacity to believe? Instead of despair, you trust in God! And somehow everything seems to go in another direction. How excellent is such a character. Let's hear how one man lived such an incredible life of believing, even during breakfast!*

"The price of bread is going up!" a man told George Müller anxiously one day. "What will you do?"

"Well," Mr. Müller replied thoughtfully, "I guess our God who can provide us with a loaf of bread that costs four pennies, can also provide us a loaf that costs eight."

This was how George Müller looked at problems. He was a believer. He trusted in prayer for everything that was needed. And trust he

*Mr. Müller recently opened three houses
full of orphans in England.*

did. For this man of faith had, at this point, recently opened three houses full of orphans in England. But, in all these years, he never asked anyone for money. That's right, not once. Even more, he did not allow any of the helpers to ask for money either. Nope. He strictly forbid them from ever asking for money or telling anyone how much, or how little, was in their account.

Now you should not think Mr. Müller was careless. No, he always wrote down an exact account of all the prayers he prayed, and all the prayers that were answered. He did this so that others could see for themselves that God is faithful, that God really does answer prayers.

In one case, a lady who owned some costly jewelry decided to give it all to Mr. Müller for the Lord to use to care for the orphans. The money that was raised from the sale of those necklaces and bracelets was enough to pay all the bills for a whole week and provide wages for the helpers as well. Before he sold one of the diamond rings, Mr. Müller used it to etch a little message on a glass window. "Jehovah Jireh," he wrote. In Hebrew this means: "The Lord will provide." Whenever there were problems after that, George just looked at that writing on the window and was encouraged to keep believing in the God who loves to provide.

And so, there was always food to eat and clothes to wear. The children in the homes never had any idea that some days there was hardly any money to buy anything. Only Mr. Müller and the workers knew that. And to remedy that every time, they would join Mr. Müller in his

Mr. Müller etched a little message on a glass window: "The Lord will provide."

prayers of faith. Sometimes, when they had no money to pay the bills, Mr. Müller would go for a long walk to pray, and sometimes a complete stranger would stop him on the street and give him just enough money to pay for the orphans' next meal. Then, Mr. Müller would simply go on his way, up the street, rejoicing.

But this morning was especially hard. You see, this morning, there was no food in the kitchen, and there was no money left to purchase any. And to make it worse, 300 hungry little orphans were taking their seats at the tables in Mr. Müller's orphanage to eat breakfast—a breakfast that they just didn't have. As Mr. Müller came down to the room, he was well aware of the dire situation. Hundreds of hungry mouths waited with nothing to prepare for them. But, exercising to believe the God who provides, he confidently took the hand of one of the little children who was visiting the orphanage that day, and leading her to the table, gently said, "Come my dear. Let's see what our Father will do."

So there they were with the tables all set for breakfast. All the cups and bowls and utensils were laid neatly in their places. The 300 children were also there, sitting and waiting in their appointed seats, looking expectantly at the empty dishes before them. Then, as they did every morning, they bowed their heads and closed their eyes as Mr. Müller began to pray in front of them, thanking the Lord for the food.

"Dear Father," he prayed, "we thank You for what You are about to give us to eat—"

*The 300 children were
waiting in their appointed seats.*

Suddenly, a loud knock from the back door interrupted him. He paused and turned to the door. Again, there was knocking. Mr. Müller walked over and opened the door slowly. To everyone's surprise, there was the local baker! He was standing there in the doorway looking very tired and anxious!

"Mr. Müller, sir, please, sir, I just couldn't sleep at all last night. I had the feeling that you and the children needed bread for your breakfast this morning and that the Lord wanted me to bring you some to you all. So, I rose up very early this morning, at 2 o'clock, to bake all this bread for you."

And with that, the baker delivered enough bread for everyone. Mr. Müller smiled, thanked the kind man, and praised the Lord for His unfailing care. It was a very special thing indeed for them to have fresh, warm bread such as this for breakfast.

Suddenly, there was another knock at the door. This time, it was the milk man. He was all flustered and out of breath. To everyone's surprise, they saw his milk cart had broken down right outside the orphanage!

"Mr. Müller," the man gasped. "Look! My milk cart has broken down right here. I'm afraid all my milk will spoil before my cart can be repaired. Do you think it would be possible for me to give you these 10 large cans of fresh milk for the orphans?"

Amazing! Where there had been no food at all in the home only a few minutes ago, now, the children's plates and cups were filled with warm bread and fresh milk. Surely this was all the Lord's timely provi-

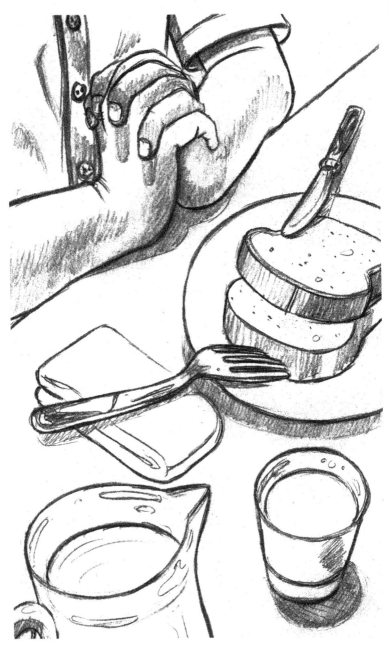

*The children's plates and cups were filled
with warm bread and fresh milk.*

sion. I think you would agree as well, that this was surely an unforgettable breakfast with Mr. Müller.

For this reason I say to you,
All things that you pray and ask,
believe that you have received them,
and you will have them.

MARK 11:24

For more children's stories, songs, videos, crafts, and activities please visit us online.

Standing on the Bible and Growing!

67389498R00047

Made in the USA
San Bernardino, CA
23 January 2018